by
Charis Mather

Minneapolis, Minnesota

Credits
All images are courtesy of Shutterstock.com, unless otherwise specified. With thanks to Getty Images, Thinkstock Photo, and iStockphoto.

Recurring images – Cute vector illustration, Yauhen Paleski, Random Illustrator, Iyeyee. Cover – Zaie, 4thDesign, VovanIvanovich. 4–5 – Macrovector, Denis Andricic, RIMM_Art, tomertu, umarazak. 6–7 – Digital Storm, M.KOS, Marben. 8–9 – mrjo2405, N. F. Photography, lukpedclub, sakmeniko. 10–11 – Georgina198, Alfmaler, ArtMari, T Studio, Wellcome Images (WikimediaCommons). 12–13 – Anne Coatesy, CoreyFord, stockakia, Catmando. 14–15 – fabiofoto, Mariana Serdynska, PhotoRK, Sergnester, Tohuwabohu1976. 16–17 – Firn, ilovezion, 4zevar, Dotted Yeti. 18–19 – Digital Storm, Hi-Point, song138 Mr. Tickle (Wikimedia Commons). 20–21 – Domenichino (Wikimedia Commons), Animation Dina, Francey. 22–23 – UfaBizPhoto, Krakenimages.com.

Bearport Publishing Company Product Development Team
President: Jen Jenson; Director of Product Development: Spencer Brinker; Managing Editor: Allison Juda; Associate Editor: Naomi Reich; Associate Editor: Tiana Tran; Senior Designer: Colin O'Dea; Associate Designer: Elena Klinkner; Associate Designer: Kayla Eggert; Product Development Assistant: Owen Hamlin

Library of Congress Cataloging-in-Publication Data

Names: Mather, Charis, 1999- author.
Title: Unicorns / by Charis Mather.
Description: Fusion books. | Minneapolis, Minnesota : Bearport Publishing Company, 2024. | Series: Mythical creatures | Includes index.
Identifiers: LCCN 2023032413 (print) | LCCN 2023032414 (ebook) | ISBN 9798889163053 (library binding) | ISBN 9798889163107 (paperback) | ISBN 9798889163145 (ebook)
Subjects: LCSH: Unicorns--Juvenile literature.
Classification: LCC GR830.U6 M (print) | LCC GR830.U6 (ebook) | DDC 398/.469--dc23/eng/20230721
LC record available at https://lccn.loc.gov/2023032413
LC ebook record available at https://lccn.loc.gov/2023032414

© 2024 BookLife Publishing
This edition is published by arrangement with BookLife Publishing.

North American adaptations © 2024 Bearport Publishing Company. All rights reserved. No part of this publication may be reproduced in whole or in part, stored in any retrieval system, or transmitted in any form or by any means, electronic, mechanical, photocopying, recording, or otherwise, without written permission from the publisher.

For more information, write to Bearport Publishing, 5357 Penn Avenue South, Minneapolis, MN 55419.

CONTENTS

Myths, Magic, and More. **4**
What Does a Unicorn Look Like? **6**
The Horn **8**
Healing Powers **10**
This and That **12**
A Unicorn's Meal **14**
Where Unicorns Live **16**
Mythical Look-Alikes **18**
Real-Life Unicorns? **20**
Mysterious Mythical Creatures **22**
Glossary **24**
Index **24**

MYTHS, MAGIC, AND MORE

Most people have heard of the horned magical beasts known as unicorns. But you probably haven't seen one in real life. Why not? Because unicorns are **mythical** creatures!

For thousands of years, people from all around the world have told stories about unicorns. Different **legends** talk about the creatures in different ways. Let's learn what the stories have to say!

In Latin, the word *unicorn* means having one horn.

WHAT DOES A UNICORN LOOK LIKE?

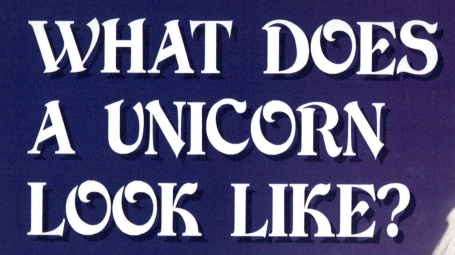

Let's take a closer look at these single-horned beasts.

Beard

Some say unicorns have long hair under their chins a lot like goats.

THE HORN

One of the most amazing things about unicorns is their horns! Without horns, unicorns would look just like horses.

Early legends said the unicorn's horn was colored. The tip was red. The middle of the horn was said to be black, and the bottom was white. Now, many stories say they are all white.

Horns help animals protect themselves. Some animals, such as sheep, have horns made of bone. If unicorns were real, maybe their horns would help them fight.

Some animal horns are made of the same stuff as what is in our hair and nails.

HEALING POWERS

In addition to having horns, many people say unicorns may have healing powers!

In stories, unicorns can **purify** poisoned water. All they need to do is dip their horns in the water! Then, it becomes safe for other animals to drink.

In the past, some people said they found unicorn horns. Sometimes, they would turn them into cups. Drinking from these cups was thought to protect from **disease**. Other people crushed the horns into a powder that was used to heal.

Unicorn horn powder

THIS AND THAT

A group of unicorns is called a blessing. This is the same as the name given to a group of narwhals, underwater creatures with hornlike **tusks**.

Many unicorns are said to have white bodies. This is thought to show they are pure creatures.

Many people say white lambs are also pure.

A UNICORN'S MEAL

Like horses, unicorns are said to eat grass and hay. They may also like fruits, such as apples. Some stories say they feed on flowers and leaves!

In some tales, unicorns eat rainbows! Could each color of the rainbow taste different?

People say unicorns drink water from rivers and streams like other animals.

WHERE UNICORNS LIVE

Some legends say unicorns live in thick forests. They may also be found near rivers.

Some **myths** say seeing a unicorn means something good will happen.

In stories, unicorns are not often seen by people. When they are, they are very hard to catch!

MYTHICAL LOOK-ALIKES

There are other mythical creatures like unicorns. Let's look at a few.

Qilin horn

A qilin

Qilins are creatures from Chinese myths. Like unicorns, qilins have horns on their foreheads. **Scales** cover their bodies.

Pegasus

Pegasus is a mythical animal that looks similar to a unicorn. But Pegasus doesn't have a horn. Instead, he has wings to help him fly!

REAL-LIFE UNICORNS?

Where do stories of unicorns come from? Maybe from real animals. . . .

Narwhals

A narwhal has a long tusk that looks like a horn. Narwhal tusks can grow up to 10 feet (3 m) long.

Rhinoceroses

Rhinoceroses have horns on their noses rather than their foreheads. If they lose their horns, rhinos can grow them back!

MYSTERIOUS MYTHICAL CREATURES

Unicorns are fun, mysterious creatures. We can learn a lot from stories about these single-horned beasts.

If you can't get enough of unicorns, just read some books! There is so much to explore about these mythical creatures.

GLOSSARY

disease a sickness or illness

legends stories from the past that may have a mix of truth and made-up things

mythical based on stories or something made up in the imagination

myths old stories that tell of strange or magical events and creatures

purify to make something clean and safe

scales small, hard skin parts found on animals such as fish and snakes

tusk a long, pointed tooth

INDEX

blessing 12
goat 6
horns 4–11, 18–19, 21–22
horse 8, 14
narwhals 12, 21
Pegasus 19
poison 10
powers 7, 10
pure 13
qilins 18
rhinoceroses 21
wings 19